Women's Prosperity Ne[...] Experts Compilation Bo[...]

15 WPN Business Professionals Share Essential Information on Areas of Their Expertise

In this amazing Itty Bitty™ book fifteen WPN experts combine to provide you with information about:

- Sandra Jo Aletraris - Seeds to Succeed When Healing is in Need
- Leiah Kerns Carr - Visualize To Success
- Peg Duchesne - Remove the Mystery of Marketing
- Shari Edgell – Do You Have a Bad Relationship with Stress and Uncertainty?
- Joy Harris - Discover the Leader Within
- Barbara Johnson - It's Your Money, So Keep It
- Christine Lennips - Causes for Lack of Energy
- Cara Nusinov - You Can Have Joy At Any Age
- Tom Rohrer - Peak Performing Athletes
- Ann Schiebert – Ridding Negative Self-Talk
- Madeleine Sklar - The Benefits of an Ancient Wisdom Empowerment Reading
- Sue Tabaka-Kritzeck - Claim Your Charisma!
- Rita Thomas - Every Business Needs a CRM
- Alexandra Van Horn - The Science Behind the Law of Attraction
- Judy Yates - Cutting Loose and Going Mobile

If you are interested in learning more about these beneficial topics pick up a copy of this must-read Itty Bitty™ book today; meet our authors and expand your knowledge.

Your Amazing Itty Bitty™ WPN Experts Compilation Book
Volume II

15 Chapters by WPN Professionals who Share Essential Information on Areas of Their Expertise

Sandra Jo Aletraris

Leiah Kerns Carr

Peg Duchesne

Shari Edgell

Joy Harris

Barbara Johnson

Christine Lennips

Cara Nusinov

Tom Rohrer, Ph.D.

Dr. Ann Schiebert

Madeleine Sklar

Sue Tabaka-Kritzeck

Rita Thomas

Alexandra Van Horn

Judy Yates

Published by Itty Bitty™ Publishing
A subsidiary of S & P Productions, Inc.

Printed in the United States of America

Itty Bitty Publishing
311 Main Street, Suite D
El Segundo, CA 90245
(310) 640-8885

ISBN: 978-1-959964-96-4

Dedications

Sandra Jo Aletraris: This chapter is dedicated to dear friends and family who extended a powerful hope line of love to my family and me by their outpouring of care, prayers and unending love to rebuild from the ruins of a suicidal loss.

Leiah Kerns Carr: To my loving husband, and best friend, Sean, and my amazing children, Scott and Lauren, daughter-in-law, Elizabeth, and sister, Leilani. I love you all forever and always! And in honor of my Dad and Mom who taught me; I could do anything I put my mind to.

Peg Duchesne: To the visionary entrepreneurs and dedicated business professionals who placed their trust in our collaborative journey. Your partnership not only fuels my growth but also inspires my work each day. Thank you for allowing me to be a part of your success.

Shari Edgell: I would like to dedicate my pages in gratitude for all that God has done to redeem the many trials I have been through to be in a place where I can now help others. And I am forever grateful to my David who has been my needed support on my journey.

Joy Harris: Dedicated to women who found an opportunity to lead but have felt doubt creep in. Let your leadership and confidence muscles strengthen so you can radiate wisdom to others. You can shine your light out into the world when you believe in yourself.

Barbara Johnson: I dedicate this chapter to the children in my life, those I have helped raise, and those around the world whom I have "adopted" to improve their life circumstances and give them a better foundation so they, too, can succeed in the world on their terms.

Christine Lennips For my parents who started me on my journey to health. For my husband who is such a support to me in my life and with my business! To my clients who have been with me over the past 36 years. I am excited for those I will meet and help in the future!

Cara Nusinov: Dedicated to my loving children, grandchildren, good men, women of iron and lace, those who reach out a hand and those who strive for joy and peace.

Tom Rohrer, Ph.D.: I dedicate my chapter to all athletes who fully commit their time, focus and resources to becoming the best they can be; and to the fans who cheer for them, the family and friends who support them and the coaches who assist them.

Dr. Ann Schiebert: I dedicate my chapter to all you folks who talk to yourselves in a critical, inaccurate way. Remember, you were not born with negative self-talk. It's time to be truthful and kind to yourself. Learn your attributes. Here I wish for you to do just that.

Madeleine Sklar: This chapter, my life and all I do, is dedicated to Love: To all whom I love, all that I love, including my family, the Ancient Grandmothers, the Holy Presence that permeates everything. Also, writers: Joshuah Henderson, Ruth Wire and Jane Perkins.

Sue Tabaka-Kritzeck: To all the people who believe they are not enough, and that they will never have the confidence or charisma to be that person to others. Believe. You are enough. You are confident. You are charismatic.

Rita Thomas: I dedicate this chapter to all the brave souls who took the leap into entrepreneurship. There's nothing like it; we are kindred spirits and I'm honored to be walking this path with you! Special thanks to my forever love, Always on R&R.

Alexandra Van Horn: For Gregory, Ryan, Christian and their families, and all those who have come before me that lit the torch of awareness of the quantum world! To anyone who has dreamed a dream and made it happen! They have fanned the glowing embers of creation! Amen!

Judy Yates: Dedicated to my family, friends and clients who join me now virtually on my journey.

Stop by our Itty Bitty™ website to find interesting information from our WPN Experts

www.IttyBittyPublishing.com

Or visit Our Experts at

Sandra Jo Aletraris
Sandy.Jo.thornton@gmail.com

Leiah Kerns Carr
https://LeiahCarr.com

Peg Duchesne
https://duchessllc.com

Shari Edgell
www.theblessing.blog

Joy Harris
https://www.joycanhelp.com

Barbara Johnson
Barbara.johnson@kisbaa.com

Christine Lennips
https://www.knocard.app/itsaboutyou

Cara Nusinov
https://carascreativecircle.com

Tom Rohrer, Ph.D.
www.peakperformancescorecard.com

Dr. Ann Schiebert
http://drannschiebert.com/

Madeleine Sklar
madeleine@grandmothershealingwisdom.com

Sue Tabaka-Kritzeck
www.yourfascinationfactor.com

Rita Thomas
www.RitaThomasEnterprises.com

Alexandra Van Horn
www.avhcoaching.com

Judy Yates
www.jyatescpa.com/resources

Table of Contents

Introduction

Are you trying to keep up in this hectic, fast-paced world? Between checking emails, staying on top of social media, handling all the demands of daily life, AND running a business – whew, it will make you want to throw your hands up and surrender sometimes!

That's why the Women's Prosperity Network community exists and that's why we compiled these profound, life-enhancing wisdom bombs so that you can be the powerful force that you truly are. I'm talking upgrades that will transform your approach to work and life itself. This book is your invitation to reclaim your time, energy and sanity once and for all. To stop just going through the motions and say "Hello!" to living fully and fiercely in peak alignment with your highest purpose.

You'll hear from the heavyweights, high-powered CEOs, and trusted authorities leading the revolution in life. You'll also learn from the sweet souls putting these lessons into practice day in, day out, and the take-no-excuses mamas juggling kids and work; the passionate, hard-working women blazing their own trails. They've tried it all and brought back the hard-won gems just for you.

The path ahead is lit by the experiences of incredible go-getters who walked this road before you. Their insights, shortcuts and clever tools are all right here, ready to unfold a new way of doing life. More ease, more grace, more of that light you were born to radiate, shining fully.

So get ready! Roll up those sleeves, take a deep breath and prepare to hack your days with elegance and tenacity. Because from here on out, you're going to live fully awakened to your greatness.

Our deepest fear is not that we are inadequate.
Our deepest fear is that we are
powerful beyond measure.
~Marianne Williamson
"A Return to Love"

Women's Prosperity Network is a movement, a sisterhood – of women (and a few good men) coming together to be the best we can be so that with our products, our projects and our services make a massive positive difference in the world.

To learn more, go to WomensProsperityNetwork.com.

Trish Carr
Co-Founder of Women's Prosperity Network

Expert 1
Sandra Jo Aletraris
Seeds to Succeed When Healing is in Need

Has a horrible loss struck your heart and home?
Losing a loved one to suicide is shattering. Here
you will find groundbreaking words that fortify
seeds of truth, to transform something painful
into something healing. These words will give
you solace.

Identify your pain points which diminish peace
and joy at the core of your heart:

1. Agonizing with unanswered whys
2. Overwhelmed with grief and lost dreams
3. Unforgiveness of self and judgment
4. Self-condemnation and rejection
5. Fearful and distracted by uncertainties
6. Shame and abandonment

Big things come in small packages and the seeds
that are sown here will spark your heart to refresh
your soul, recover your faith, and restore your
joy! It's time to start planting new seeds that
bring new fruit and much better outcomes:

1. Seek a safe place for guidance
2. Expose the enemy of your soul
3. Rebuild your worth, alignment, love, and
   laughter

Seeds are to the Soil as Your Faith is for the Heart

- Invite Spirit into your pain through prayer or meditation.
- Spend time reading the words of your spiritual belief.
- Destroy your need to question, "What if?"
- Take note of every thought that brings words, actions, and habits. This sets your character and your destiny.
- Forgive yourself, others, and God to experience the grip of grief and turn it into grace.
- Grow your spiritual faith.

What you sow in the healing process is what you'll reap in the garden of your heart. Your spiritual practice provides you with renewed strength, confidence, and new adventures.

- Create a space in your home to connect with your spiritual practice.
- Learn how to connect on a deeper level.
- Seek out community and enjoy friendships with those of similar beliefs, experiences, and interests.

For more information contact Sandra Jo Aletraris at Sandy.Jo.thornton@gmail.com

Expert 2
Leiah Kerns Carr
Visualize Your Way to Success

Visualization is a powerful tool that you can use to impact your journey to success. By understanding the power of visualization, you will be equipped with a tool that can help shape and manifest your future.

Visualization can help you:

1. Define your goals and aspirations.
2. Identify and overcome obstacles and build resilience.
3. Cultivate a positive, success mindset.

The practice of visualization is not only a powerful technique for achieving personal goals and success but also has a scientific basis rooted in how the brain functions. When you engage in visualization, your brain activates similar neural pathways as when you actually experience the imagined scenario.

Visualization stimulates or activates:

1. Your brain's emotional centers, such as the amygdala and prefrontal cortex.
2. Your reticular activating system tells the brain what you want to focus on achieving your goals.

More on Visualizing Your Way to Success

Visualization also enhances motivation by tapping into the brain's reward system. When you visualize achieving a goal or experiencing success, your brain releases neurotransmitters such as dopamine, which is associated with pleasure and motivation. This neurochemical response reinforces your neural pathways making you more driven to take actions that bring you closer to your goals. By harnessing the power of visualization, you can:

- Influence your brain functioning
- Reduce your stress
- Enhance your overall well-being

Embracing visualization on a regular basis can lead to significant positive changes in your brain and empower you to achieve your goals and success. Visualization helps you:

- Increase your confidence
- Cultivate a success-oriented mindset
- Foster a sense of abundance and possibility

To discover more success, mindset and manifesting courses, products and tips visit:
https://leiahcarr.com

Expert 3
Peg Duchesne
Remove the Mystery of Marketing

A digital marketing strategy is crucial for success. Establish clear and compelling content themes. Laser-focus your efforts and create high-quality, consistent messaging. Simplify your marketing efforts.

1. Have a focused approach.
2. Demonstrate your authority and expertise.
3. Focus resources and creativity around a single theme per month.

Streamline your process by repurposing content. Rather than creating entirely new content for each channel, adapt and repurpose your core content to suit different platforms, including:

1. Blog posts
2. Social media posts
3. Infographics
4. Videos
5. Newsletters

More About Removing the Mystery of Marketing

This focused approach simplifies content creation and facilitates the seamless repurposing of content across different platforms. As a result, you will find that your marketing efforts become more effective, efficient and ultimately, more successful.

Implementing this strategy has these outcomes:

- Ensures your message reaches a wider and more appropriate and receptive audience.
- Enables you to maximize the impact of your marketing efforts and maintain consistent brand identity across your various platforms.

For more information visit Peg Duchesne at:
https://duchessllc.com

Expert 4
Shari Edgell, LPC
Do You Have a Bad Relationship with Stress and Uncertainty?

Most people have a bad relationship with stress that creates a worry/anxiety cycle to try and reduce stress. A hidden culprit is fueling the stress and that culprit is the Intolerance of Uncertainty (IU). Here is how it feeds off of stress:

1. You have stressors.
2. You develop IU and may not believe in your ability to cope.
3. Worry becomes a mechanism to try to gain control (I must make the uncertain certain!).
4. This pattern creates anxiety.

This anxiety leads you to one of two responses (or a mix of the two):

1. You think you can control so you obsess, strive for perfection, overplan, get busy, become rigid, and maybe angry.
2. You can't get control so you procrastinate, distract, isolate, ignore, avoid, deny, and maybe get depressed.

Both of these responses actually increase stress not decrease it!

Doing Relationship Work

If you resonate with any of this, you have a bad relationship with stress and uncertainty. As with most bad relationships, you can end, tolerate, or fix them. The first page is about trying to end things with uncertainty in a new relationship with "Certainty" (not always possible). Freedom comes through learning to embrace uncertainty. That is quite a leap from IU so start here:

- Recall the goodness you have experienced in the past
- Believe in your ability to cope
- Use your five senses to stay present
- Create a list of gratitude big to small

The next step is to say the following:

- "I know what I need to know right now!"
- Focus on what is going well in your life right now

Through this, you will be better able to embrace uncertainty! Next, figure out:

- What I wish I could control
- What I can't control
- What I can control

Work with what you can control and make a flexible plan!

For more information, visit
www.theblessing.blog

Expert 5
Joy Harris, Success Coach
Discover the Leader Within

Are you recognized as a leader? Have you achieved leadership status, but your ideas get overlooked and you are not getting the attention and respect you deserve? Believe in yourself!

Leaders are recognized for three powerful skills:

1. *Communication* Skills.
2. *Clarity* on presentations and proposals.
3. *Confidence* in presenting your ideas and demonstrating that you are the one who can follow through on them to success.

Even when you are of an equal rank to others in the room, you must be able to communicate with your peers and your teammates clearly or you can miss out on getting support for your ideas.

Many women have experienced a time when their presentation was dismissed with a negative comment, and it caused them to lose confidence to continue or to speak up at the next meeting.

As a businesswoman, you sometimes shy away from being your own best cheerleader. That doesn't work anymore! Blast your own horn!

Essential Leadership Skills

Communication: Be an Ally; Gain an Ally

- Tell others you value their opinion before the next meeting.
- Share one point with them to help them understand and get their reaction.
- Offer to give them feedback or support.

You are likely to gain an ally of both women and men if you speak one-on-one prior to presenting your idea, which builds leadership skills throughout the team.

Clarity: Make Your Point Clearly

- Provide metrics to prove your point.
- Show that you have done your research.
- Present the benefits of your idea and the pitfalls if it is not implemented.

Confidence:

- You cannot teach confidence; you draw it out. You can learn to believe in yourself.
- Everyone is a leader at something, use your strengths and announce your wins.
- Learn the powers of inner strength and self-talk to exude confidence and get respect. Don't give your power away if one person disagrees. Continue, be bold.

https://www.joycanhelp.com

Expert 6
Barbara Johnson
It's Your Money, So Keep It

In the business realm, profit is essential, yet many entrepreneurs struggle to achieve it. The Profit First system challenges traditional accounting, making profit a priority rather than an after-thought.

1. Embrace the Profit First mindset. Profit becomes the primary focus, necessitating a foundational shift in your perspective. You want to prioritize profit in your earnings.
2. The system contrasts traditional accounting. Instead of the usual formula: Sales – Expenses = Profit; the formula you will use is: Sales – Profit = Expenses. This ensures you immediately allocate money to profit.
3. A hallmark of this approach is that you allocate funds across multiple bank accounts, where each one is designated for specific expenses: profit, taxes, owner's compensation, and operating expenses. This streamlines financial management.
4. Make periodic reviews and adjustments. This is vital to ensure you are aligning with your business and financial goals.

Let Me Show You How

The problem with the traditional mindset to accounting:

- Profit is at the end of the equation leading to the unfortunate scenario where businesses operate tirelessly only to find little to no profit left after everything else.
- No matter how much money you make, expenses will expand to use all of it, leaving nothing for profit.

The power of allocating your money lies in directing your funds with intention and precision. This is done with five pivotal bank accounts. These accounts ensure a structured and purposeful distribution of your funds, optimizing your financial management.

- Income Account
- Profit Account
- Owner's Compensation
- Taxes
- Operating Expense (OPEX)

For more information email me at: Barbara.johnson@kisbaa.com, or book a call: https://kisbaa.com/book-with-me/.

Expert 7
Christine Lennips
Root Causes for Lack of Energy

What are your health symptoms? You need to look beneath and beyond them. What is the root cause of the way that you feel?

Lack of energy is a common complaint. Did you know that it could relate to one or more of five different body systems?

1. Digestive system: The way that your body breaks down food so that you can absorb the nutrients from it.
2. Circulatory system: How blood moves around in your body. Consider the feelings of cold hands and feet or feeling warm far too often.
3. Immune system: This helps fight off diseases, such as bacteria and viruses, even the common cold.
4. Glandular system: Adrenals, thyroid, parathyroid, pancreas, pituitary, pineal, hypothalamus, reproductive organs.
5. Hepatic system: Liver, gall bladder, blood, detoxification.

As you seek to understand the root cause of why you don't have the energy levels that you want, remember that these five interconnected body systems shape your vitality.

More About Lack of Energy

Some options to help boost your energy levels.

Digestive System - You will benefit from:

- Chewing your food thoroughly!
- Papaya, ginger, digestive enzymes

Circulatory System - You will benefit from:

- Drinking 6+ 8 oz. glasses of water a day, exercise/move your body
- Cayenne, ginkgo, hawthorn

Immune System - You will benefit from:

- Keep your bowels moving, wash hands
- Echinacea, astragalus, elderberry

Glandular System - You will benefit from:

- Take breaks throughout your day, good sleep, maintain a healthy body weight
- Kelp, evening primrose oil, ginseng

Hepatic System - You will benefit from:

- Gently detoxify in the Spring and Fall
- Milk thistle, dandelion, turmeric

Five other body systems could need support.

For more information visit
https://www.knocard.app/itsaboutyou

Expert 8
Cara Nusinov
You Can Have Joy at Any Age:
Tame Your Monkey Mind

Are you asking, "Are all of my life's adventures all in the past?" "What can help me control negative thoughts?"

Negative thoughts, sometimes called Monkey Mind, are a restlessness, confusion or maybe perhaps, your inner critic.

How can you feel natural joy? Why not ask, "What adventures still lie before me?"

1. You are never too old to have adventures.
2. Does your mind give you reasons for not having those adventures? That's your Monkey Mind, and it needs a new job!
3. Take action. Yes, action. Notice the things that are working for you.

Then, LAUGH.

More About that "Monkey Mind"

Laughter is the greatest elixir for changing your mental state.

Laugh more every day. While you are actively laughing you'll find it challenging to have negative thoughts. It's difficult to be sad, confused, upset, or even angry when you are laughing.

Once you start the physical act of laughter, the brain cannot tell if you are faking it, and you'll feel more joy.

- You may release serotonin, a laughter hormone. After you brush your teeth look in the mirror and say, "haha hoho," and start laughing, or while washing dishes, or each time you end a phone call.
- You can release your creativity. You may feel silly in the beginning, but that's okay, just laugh aloud, fake it, till you make it.
- Meditate and become still to find some peace and relaxation. It will soon become a habit and something you look forward to.
- Celebrate yourself.

For more information contact me at Joyful Laughter at The Serotonin Express and Cara's Laughter Lounge, through a private message on FB or email: frommywindowbycara@yahoo.com or my website: carascreativecircle.com

Expert 9
Tom Rohrer, Ph.D.
Becoming a Peak Performing Athlete

The acronym S.P.O.R.T.S. summarizes my model for assisting average athletes to become their very best, and, with some talent, elite athletes. It stands for:

1. Superior
2. Performances...come when you
3. Offset...or eliminate the negative
4. Repeat...successful patterns
5. Tap...into your personal resources
6. Stay...in the present moment and flow state

There are commonly used resources that can help you improve your performance, such as affirmations, mental imagery, cognitive restructuring, and reminders. Two other highly effective tools are:

1. Brainspotting
2. The Play Zone

Brainspotting[1]: is a neurobiological approach that assists your brain and body to work for you, in a laser-like manner, to process issues and self-heal.

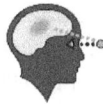

---

[1] Brainspotting, developed by David Grand, Ph.D.

More on These Two Highly Effective Tools

Brainspotting makes use of the phenomenon that "Where you look affects how you feel." The three ways Brainspotting can assist you are to:

- Offset…or eliminate your negative past. Quickly and easily resolve the emotional intensity of past painful experiences, which can be the cause of mental blocks and slumps.
- Tap…into your personal resources. Find and utilize your inner resources, such as calmness, courage or mental toughness.
- Stay…in the present and in the flow state. Being in a flow or "zone" state maximizes your ability and results.

The Play Zone[2]: is a science-backed, polyvagal informed approach. It uses self-awareness of your body to manage your fight-flight-freeze reaction and direct your mental-emotional-physical state for peak performance. In the process, you get to:

- Stay…in the present moment and flow state
- Build a sense of safety and connection
- Perform in "play zone" with relaxed activation, while building resiliency.

For more information visit Dr. Tom at www.peakperformancescorecard.com or www.tomrohrer.com

---

[2] The Play Zone, developed by Michael Allison

Expert 10
Ann Schiebert, PsyD
Getting Rid of Negative Self-Talk

Many people unconsciously adopt negative self-talk because these are the sentences that have been said to them over and over at various times in their lives. Physiologically, your negative self-talk turns on your sympathetic nervous system and leads to exhaustion. Extinguishing belittling chatter will assist with increased self-esteem, help with less anxiety and give a more accurate assessment of who you are as a person.

Where Does Negative Self-Talk Come From?

1. Introjects: Unconscious adoption of negative statements about yourself.
2. Shame: Manifested by negative feelings about yourself.
3. Comparison: Thinking that someone else is better than you are.

What Does Negative Self-Talk Do to Your Body?

1. It puts you in fight, flight or freeze mode.
2. You feel unconscious/conscious fear.
3. Your kidneys spew adrenaline.
4. It puts your body in a constant state of "red alert."

How to Get Rid of Negative Self-Talk

Know your values and don't let yourself or others violate them.

- Label and express emotions.
- Let go of thinking it is your responsibility to offset other people's anger.
- Make a list of the negative things you tell yourself and determine if your denigrating chatter is accurate or if it is what someone told you about yourself.
- Explore your boundaries and know what they are. Are you a people pleaser who fears the anger of others so you ignore limits?
- Polyvagal exercises help calm the vagus nerve which gets disrupted by trauma and anxiety. These exercises will assist you in calming your sympathetic nervous system and help you calm your body. Find them on YouTube and DO them.
- Positive and true affirmations that you repeatedly practice will eventually take the place of your negative self-talk.
- Create a meaningful and true self-narrative.
- Develop ease with self-imperfections.
- Acquire compassion for yourself.

For more information go to
drannschiebert.com

Expert 11
Madeleine Sklar, MS
The Benefits of an
Ancient Wisdom Empowerment Reading

Ancestral wisdom is woven into the very cells of your being. It is waiting for you. Waiting to be recovered and brought into the light of your consciousness. While only the Holy One can predict, create, and determine your fate, an Ancient Wisdom Empowerment Reading can reveal your unconscious gifts and blocks and prepare you to anticipate and overcome upcoming challenges. Once you're aware of your, often unconscious, gifts and influences, you are better equipped to set your path and fulfill your life's purpose.

1. If your life has changed or is about to change, it can clarify and reveal hidden perspectives, and motivations so you can make better choices.
2. You'll gain tools to help you navigate your way to a rewarding new chapter.
3. It helps you access your innate creativity inner knowing and soul purpose.
4. A relationship reading can help you better understand the dynamics of your relationship.

Ancient Wisdom Empowerment Readings Versus Tarot

Tarot originated in patriarchal Renaissance Europe. It mashed Arabic numerals, Christian and Greek archetypes, with the 9,000-year-old numeric/ideographic letters of the mystical sacred Hebrew alphabet created by the Goddess worshiping cultures of the Fertile Crescent.

- These Ancients, like science since Einstein, understood time (past, present and future) was simultaneous, not linear.
- The Hebrew Torah was described by scientist Greg Branden as "a map of quantum possibilities," a predictive source even today.
- Ancient Wisdom Empowerment Readings are drawn from the ideographic/numeric meanings hidden in the Hebrew alphabet and Tree of Life.
- As a predictive system, it helps you perceive the direction, you're moving in. You always have a choice that will take you in a new direction so predicted events can be altered or even averted and you can enjoy your success in life and relationships you desire.

For more information email me at:
madeleine@grandmothershealingwisdom.com

Expert 12
Sue Tabaka-Kritzeck
Claim Your Charisma!

Someone walks into the room, and everyone's head turns. People smile and appear to be captivated. They are magnetically drawn to that person. That's CHARISMA, a quality that some think others are born with. Not so! Just as with confidence and public speaking, charisma is a skill you can learn and practice. And it starts with being authentic.

1. Understand what makes you different from others. Hone that uniqueness so that it shines through in everything you say and do. Your authenticity shines through.
2. Exercise your confidence muscle every day until it is as strong as it can be. Be an active listener and an effective communicator; two essential components for being charismatic and confident.
3. Recognize your influence. As you project your warmth and enthusiasm when connecting with others, practice empathy and emotional intelligence. Be genuinely curious about others and show your support and encouragement to them.
4. Smile with your eyes!

Exercising Your Charisma Muscle

Think of both charisma and confidence as muscles that you can strengthen if you exercise them—just as you exercise your body to stay in good physical shape.

- Show your passion and enthusiasm for what you do
- Display optimism and positive energy
- Practice smiling and maintaining eye contact when speaking with others
- Maintain positive, open body language

Exercising Your Confidence Muscle

- Ask questions
- Empower yourself and others
- Show interest in others and listen for commonalities to strengthen your connections
- Engage others through motivation
- Practice cultivating a growth mindset

For more information, visit
www.yourfascinationfactor.com

Expert 13
Rita Thomas, Funnel Godmother
Every Business Needs a CRM

CRM stands for Client Relationship Manager, a computer software program that stores and organizes your leads, prospects, clients, affiliates, vendors, and joint venture partners. A great CRM will have many of the following features:

1. Tagging Ability with Category Distinctions
2. Scanning Business Cards Directly Into the CRM
3. Phone Integration (keeps track of phone call dates, length, and reason for the call)
4. Autoresponders; Automatic Email and Text Sending; Automatic Task Tracking
5. Mobile App (to take your business with you when out of the office)
6. Online Calendar (for easy appointment booking)
7. Landing Pages to Collect New Leads
8. Integrated Payment Portal (so you can get paid!)
9. Group Email and Text Sending with Delay Timers Included
10. Project and/or Sales Pipeline (for tracking progress through a process)

How to Use a CRM

The most effective and efficient use of a CRM is to segment your list, based on your client's needs, interests, and behaviors. This lets you send the right information to the right person at the right time. Here are some examples to consider:

- Sending photo session invites to local contacts (not nationwide)
- Sending termite inspection offers only to homeowners (not apartment dwellers)
- Sending restaurant coupons for "Beef Bonanza" night – excluding your vegetarian and vegan customers
- Sending invites to past masterclass attendees for the next workshop

To get you started, here are some automated sequence suggestions for most businesses:

- New Lead Follow-Up Emails
- New Customer Onboarding
- Webinar Invites and Reminders

For more information and to find out which CRM program is best for your business visit: www.RitaThomasEnterprises.com.

Expert 14
Alexandra Van Horn
The Science Behind the Law of Attraction
Is it Hocus Pocus? Or Just About Focus?

The Law of Attraction has been a popular topic for years. Some disregard it. Others believe in it wholeheartedly; believing they could focus on something they desire, and it would magically show up in their lives. This is partially true.

1. From quantum physics, we know that everything is energy. Physical objects have energy. Thoughts and feelings do as well.
2. Picture something you're grateful for like a loved one or a favorite meal. Notice your feelings. Now picture something sad. Notice your feelings. Your thoughts have energy and grateful thoughts raise your energy while sad thoughts lower it.

There is a system in the brain called the Reticular Activating System (RAS). This system works to filter out what you don't want and notices what you do want. It helps you focus and attract your desires

Here's How It Works

You raise your energy (your vibration) through the daily practice of gratitude. Next, you focus on the object of your desires often. Ideally, multiple times a day. Through imagination, you feel the feelings you would experience if your desires were already realized. This is key.

- Your RAS goes to work automatically seeking what you're looking for.
- Think: How many times have you suddenly noticed all the cars on the road that match your dream car? That's your RAS at work.

The last, and very important step is you take action. This is where many people get stuck. You still do what you can do every day to move in the direction of your dreams. So, the key steps are:

- Raise your vibration with daily gratitude.
- Notice when chance opportunities appear. (Your RAS at work!)
- Take action in the direction of your dreams.

For more information visit
www.avhcoaching.com

Expert 15
Judy Yates, CPA
Cutting Loose and Going Mobile
Breaking the Bonds that Tie You Down

Did you know you can "go mobile" and travel around the country? While keeping your travel tax deductible and staying within tax laws, you can take your business or your home on the road.

You may be of an age where you are considering retirement/semi-retirement. Or you just want to get away from the Maddening Crowd. Can You?

YES, you can. The questions you need to ask yourself include: Is this something you can afford? Can you still support yourself and leave the classic office behind?

Grab a journal and pen. Now let's get started.

1. Explore your dreams, needs and options: space needs, equipment, services
2. Set your budget, and start your search for your best fit: explore RV options
3. Follow the tax laws of the IRS and each state you work from. Know how to stay within tax laws, and even take advantage of them
4. Stop, smell the roses, and enjoy that sunset. Cut loose!

More About Cutting Loose, and Going Mobile

Ask yourself:

- Exactly what are you looking for? A home? An office? Both?
- If you want to go off-grid, how much or little space do you really need? Make a list of business and/or personal items you think are required. How will you determine what is essential?
- Budgeting and planning: Your mobile escape pod will probably involve more fuel and other costs than you expect. Are these offset by expenses you will no longer be paying? Plan for it and jump for joy as you head out on your adventure.

Read the FREE paper on my website to explore your own plan for "cutting loose", how you can go mobile, and take advantage of the tax laws from the road.

For more information visit:
www.jyatescpa.com/resources
look for 'cutting loose'

You've finished. Before you go...

Post/share that you finished this book.

Please star rate this book.

Reviews are solid gold to writers. Please take a few minutes to give us some itty bitty feedback.

ABOUT THE AUTHORS

Sandra Jo Aletraris, her three children and ten grandchildren endured the loss of her late husband to suicide. As a result, her passion now is to help rebuild families, bringing restorative health and vitality back to each member impacted by the loss of a loved one.

Leiah Kerns Carr is an author, speaker, international educator and energy healer. Also, she is a success, mindset and manifesting coach. She's known as a leader, teacher and master manifester. Leiah has been a CEO and President of multiple corporations in the wellness industry.

Peg Duchesne, the "Message Therapist," empowers entrepreneurs and professionals as a communications consultant and relationship marketing strategist. She is also a Certified B.A.N.K ™ IOS Coach who propels her clients to greater success in business and life.

ABOUT THE AUTHORS

Shari Edgell is a Licensed Professional Counselor in private practice. Some of her specialties are working with various forms of trauma, anxiety, surviving abuse and healing self-esteem. She does this through transforming thought processes and misguided beliefs into truth.

Joy Harris, Success Coach, helps women find their definition of success and reach their goals. With her stress management and business skills background, Joy empowers her clients to find strength. Her coaching inspires belief in yourself so you can move mountains.

Barbara Johnson is a Strategic Accountant with a B.A. in Accounting ('06), specializing in serving small businesses. A US Navy vet, she's certified by NACPB, AIPB and DBA and is a QuickBooks ProAdvisor. She firmly believes in maximizing your hard-earned dollars.

ABOUT THE AUTHORS

Christine Lennips is a passionate herbalist and well-being expert. For 35+ years she has been helping each of her clients get to the root cause of the health symptoms that they are experiencing. Christine offers group sessions and one-on-one consultations.

Cara Nusinov, poet, teacher and collage artist, has joyfully led workshops for decades, at The Poetry *Buffet* Party, Laughter Yoga clubs, Art Journaling, presenting original prompts, enabling participants to write original work and to laugh and meditate at any age.

Tom Rohrer, Ph.D., Mental Performance Consultant and Psychotherapist in Colorado Springs, focuses on sports performance and addiction recovery. His next book, *Beyond Peak Performance*, is due out in early 2025. His first book is, *Thriving Beyond Addiction.*

ABOUT THE AUTHORS

Dr. Ann Schiebert's experience in the Emergency room of a large HMO led to her specializing in the treatment of trauma, family/couples issues, addiction, military challenges, grief and codependency. You can hear programs from her Relationship Radio Show at drannschiebert.com.

Madeleine Sklar MS, is a Priestess, best-selling author and speaker. She employs multiple skills, including Ancient Wisdom Empowerment Readings. Her 60+ years of experience, helps people create and enjoy success in their lives and the relationships they desire.

Sue Tabaka-Kritzeck is a Confidence Trainer. Her work leads others to find their unique strengths through learning to be authentic and confident. She is the founder of Your Fascination Factor and is a certified advisor for the How to Fascinate program.

ABOUT THE AUTHORS

Rita Thomas is an Entrepreneur, Automation Specialist, Speaker and Air Force Veteran who is committed to showing entrepreneurs how to make the most of all their assets. As a Keap Certified Partner, she teaches and supports clients through automation systems.

Alexandra Van Horn is a Transformational Life Coach, Life Mastery Consultant, ordained minister, author, a former training manager at a Fortune 500 company, mom and grandma. She has successfully inspired and coached others to achieve their dreams for over twenty years.

Judy Yates, a Certified Public Accountant (CPA) has focused on quality tax preparation for small businesses and individuals since 1985. She now has a mobile lifestyle and travels the USA extensively. Her office was conceived before the pandemic and is now a reality.

If you enjoyed this Itty Bitty™ book
you might also like…

- **Your Amazing Itty Bitty™ WPN Experts Compilation Book**

- **Your Amazing Itty Bitty™ Business Experts Compilation Book**

- **Your Amazing Itty Bitty™ Health and Wellness Experts Compilation Book**

- **Your Amazing Itty Bitty™ Holistic Experts Compilation Book**

- **Your Amazing Itty Bitty™ Word Book**

Or any of the many Amazing Itty Bitty™ books available online at www.ittybittypublishing.com